CHAPTER 1

THE PUEBLO REVOLT

Some of the people who crossed the Bering land bridge settle in what is now the **American Southwest**. They find a way to survive in this dry and hot climate. They build **pueblo** homes out of the clay ground and grow food by moving water to the fields. To them, gold is the corn they harvest. In the 1500s, the **Spanish** come looking for a different kind of gold . . .

WHICH INDIANS DWELLED IN THE CLIFFS?

ANCIENT HUNTERS IN 9,000 B.C. USE CLOVIS POINTS TO KILL BIG AMERICAN ANIMALS.

ABOUT 6000 B.C. IN THE SOUTHWEST...

:Phew!: IT'S GETTING HOT. BIG ANIMALS ARE GONE.

THAT LIZARD LOOKS GOOD...

IN 1000 B.C. ...

NO MORE LIZARDS!! I'M DIGGING CANALS TO CHANNEL WATER. WE ARE FARMING!

THE NEXT STEP: AIR CONDITIONING! PIT HOUSES BLOCK THE DESERT SUN.

TODAY'S FORECAST: HEAT, NO HUMIDITY. AGAIN.

GO GATHER CORN FOR LUNCH.

IT'S 102° F OUTSIDE!

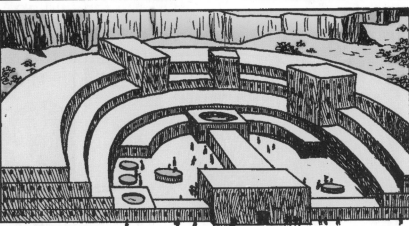

THE "ANASAZI" BUILD A BIG TRADING CENTER IN NEW MEXICO IN 1030 A.D. CRAFTSMEN IN "PUEBLO BONITO" SHAPE TURQUOISE STONES TO TRADE TO MEXICO. THIS PUEBLO (HOUSE) HAS 600 ROOMS FOR 1,000 PEOPLE.

NAVAJO AND APACHE INDIANS MOVE INTO THE SOUTHWEST. THE ANASAZI HIDE IN MESA CLIFFS FOR PROTECTION.

NICE! THESE MUD WALLS GET WARM IN THE LOW WINTER SUN, BUT THE CLIFF SHADES US IN SUMMER.

ABOUT 1300 A.D. DROUGHT HITS! FOOD SCARCITY CAUSES FIGHTS. THE ANASAZI SCATTER FROM THE CLIFFS.

next: Golden Corral

HOW DID PUEBLO INDIANS LIVE?

WHO LED THE 1680 PUEBLO REVOLT?

AFTER BEING RELEASED FROM JAIL, THE PUEBLO HOLY MAN **POPÉ** BEGINS TO ORGANIZE A REVOLT.

HOW CAN WE FIGHT THE SPANISH? WE PUEBLOS HAVE ALWAYS KEPT TO OUR OWN VILLAGES, HUNDREDS OF MILES APART!. WE DO NOT COOPERATE WITH EACH OTHER.

THE SPANISH HAVE BEEN CRUEL TO ALL OF US. THAT IS WHAT WILL UNITE US!

FOR FIVE YEARS, POPÉ SECRETLY PREACHES HIS PLAN TO PUEBLOS. NO SPANIARDS KNOW WHAT IS GOING ON UNTIL AUG. 9, 1680...

BROYD·01

GOVERNOR! A REVOLT IS PLANNED!

POPÉ! WE HAVE BEEN BETRAYED!

SEND THE SWIFTEST BOYS TO TELL EACH VILLAGE. WE ATTACK **TOMORROW!**

HMM. THERE ARE ABOUT 30,000 PUEBLOS IN NEW MEXICO. THERE ARE ONLY 2,500 OF US, SIR.

PFFT! THIS IS PROBABLY ONLY AIMED AT A FEW VILLAGES.

ON AUG. 10, 1680, PUEBLOS ACROSS NEW MEXICO ATTACK!!

WE--WE MUST GET TO THE CAPITAL NEXT! TO **SANTA FE!**

ABOUT ONE OF EVERY FIVE SPANIARDS IN NEW MEXICO IS KILLED THIS DAY. PUEBLOS BURN SPANISH CHURCHES.

DID SPANIARDS RETAKE NEW MEXICO?

THE HOLY MAN POPÉ LEADS A PUEBLO INDIAN REVOLT AGAINST THE SPANISH IN NEW MEXICO.

WE HAVE 2,000 WARRIORS. BUT THIS FORT AT SANTA FE HAS TOO MANY CANNONS!!

CUT OFF THEIR WATER SUPPLY FROM THE SANTA FE RIVER. WE WILL THIRST THEM OUT!

FOUR DAYS LATER, ON AUG. 20, 1680, THE SPANISH SURRENDER AND LEAVE.

HOW FAR DID YOU SAY IT WAS TO MEXICO CITY??

FOR 10 YEARS, NO SPANIARD SETS FOOT IN THE LAND OF THE PUEBLO INDIANS. POPÉ RULES OVER ALL THE VILLAGES.

WE WILL REBUILD OUR RELIGIOUS KIVAS!!

WE WILL WASH IN THE RIVER WITH YUCCA SUDS TO CLEAN OFF ALL SPANISH WAYS.

POPÉ DIES SEVERAL YEARS LATER. THE FEDERATION OF PUEBLO VILLAGES BREAKS APART WITHOUT HIS LEADERSHIP.

IN 1693, A SPANISH ARMY RETAKES NEW MEXICO.

SPAIN WINS, BUT ITS RULE IN NEW MEXICO IS LESS HARSH THAN WHEN IT FIRST CONTROLLED THE LAND. PUEBLOS MIX THEIR TRADITIONS WITH CHRISTIANITY — AND THEY STILL LIVE TODAY IN THE STATES OF NEW MEXICO AND ARIZONA.

WHO ROAMED THE GREAT PLAINS?

SOME ANCIENT PEOPLE WHO CROSSED THE BERING STRAIT BRIDGE LIVE ON THE GREAT PLAINS. THEY...

SHHHHH

AH!! YOU ARE NOT A WOLF!

I AM NOT LITTLE RED RIDING HOOD, EITHER. I AM TRYING TO KILL DINNER.

SSSHH

HII-YIIIII!!

A WOLFMAN!

THE BISON IS THE CENTER OF THE PLAINS INDIAN CULTURE. BISON PROVIDE FOOD AND MATERIAL FOR CLOTHING, TOOLS, AND TEEPEES. THERE ARE FEW TREES ON THIS GRASSLAND; BISON POOP EVEN FUELS FIRES!

PLAINS INDIANS FOLLOW BISON HERDS. THE PEOPLE ARE **NOMADIC**, LIVING ON THE GO. PEOPLE AND DOGS PULL FAMILY SUPPLIES ON A **TRAVOIS** (SLED).

THEN A **1680** A.D. BATTLE CAUSES SPANISH SETTLERS IN THE SOUTHWEST TO LOSE THEIR HORSES. THE HORSES MAKE IT TO THE PLAINS BY THE **1700s**. THEY CHANGE PLAINS INDIAN LIFE.

PLEASE PLEASE PLEASE DAD, CAN I HAVE ONE OF THE NEW MUSTANGS?!

THE CROW RULE!

LAKOTA!! LIVIN' LARGE!!

TRIBES CAN TRAVEL FARTHER AND PULL BIGGER TIPIS. TRIBES BATTLE TO CAPTURE HORSES FROM EACH OTHER.

END

BOYD '00

POCAHONTAS

Some of the people who cross over the Bering land bridge cross the entire North American continent. They settle among the rivers and thick forests of the **eastern woodlands**. These American Indians form the **first large-scale representative democracy** on the continent, **The Iroquois League**. And among them is a young woman named **Pocahontas**, who will be the difference between life and death for many of the first English settlers.

WHICH INDIANS LIVED IN THE EAST?

THE INDIANS LIVING IN THE EASTERN HALF OF NORTH AMERICA HAVE SIMILARITIES: FARMING CORN, SHARING POTTERY DESIGNS, LIVING IN WOOD LONG-HOUSES. BUT SOME OF THESE GROUPS STAND OUT...

THE **MOUND BUILDERS** LIVE IN THE VALLEYS OF THE **MISSISSIPPI** AND **OHIO** RIVERS. ABOUT **1000** B.C. THEY BEGIN BURYING THE DEAD IN DIRT MOUNDS.

BY **1200** A.D., AZTEC IDEAS FROM MEXICO HAVE CHANGED THESE MOUNDS INTO HOMES FOR GOD-LIKE LEADERS.

EASTERN FOREST INDIANS LIVE ALONG THE COAST OF THE **ATLANTIC OCEAN**. THEY LIVE IN THE WOODS AND HUNT DEER, CATCH FISH, AND GROW CORN.

THEIR LONGHOUSES CAN HOLD A DOZEN FAMILIES.

MOM, CAN I HAVE 23 FRIENDS OVER?

ONE FOREST GROUP IS THE **POWHATAN CONFEDERACY**. IT HAS ABOUT **10,000** PEOPLE LIVING IN **1600s** VIRGINIA.

IN THE **NORTHEAST** IS THE **IROQUOIS** GROUP. IN THE **1500s**, FIVE NATIONS JOIN INTO THE DEMOCRATIC **IROQUOIS LEAGUE**.

WE CAN LIVE IN PEACE IF WE THINK OF OUR BROTHERS' NEEDS BEFORE OUR OWN.

NEXT:
A League of Their Own

WHAT DID POCAHONTAS LIKE TO EAT?

CHESTER! DID I HEAR YOU SAY SOME ENGLISH PEOPLE FROM "THE LOST COLONY" MIGHT HAVE LIVED WITH INDIANS??

THAT IS ONE POSSIBILITY. SOME PEOPLE EVEN BELIEVE THAT ONE OF THE ENGLISHWOMEN BECAME A WIFE OF A GREAT INDIAN LEADER AND GAVE BIRTH TO POCAHONTAS.

POCAHONTAS?!!

POLKA?!

YES??

FOLLOW ME — QUICKLY! SOME SIOUAN-LANGUAGE INDIANS ARE NOT HAPPY I WANDERED ALONG THEIR TRAILS.

SO, YOUR DAD IS A ... "FIRST AMERICAN." WAS YOUR MOM A ... A EUROPEAN?

I DON'T KNOW. SHE DIED WHEN I WAS YOUNG — WHEN MY NAME WAS "MATOAKA." I WAS RAISED BY THIS VILLAGE.

POCAHONTAS' DAD IS CHIEF POWHATAN. HE HAS 100 WIVES AND 40 CHILDREN!!

SOMEONE TOLD ME MY MOM REALLY LIKED CORN.

COOL. I LIKE CORN TOO.

THIS WILL BE READY TO HARVEST SOON. IN THE WINTER WE EAT DEER AND OTHER ANIMALS FROM THE WOODS. IN THE SPRING WE EAT FISH FROM THE RIVER AND PICK BERRIES.

HER HOUSE ALSO CHANGES WITH THE SEASONS. POCAHONTAS AND OTHER EASTERN WOODLAND INDIANS LIVE IN LONGHOUSES. FIRES BURN IN THE CENTER OF THE HOUSE TO KEEP THEM WARM IN WINTER. IN THE SUMMER, SOME OF THE BARK AND GRASS COME OFF THE ROOF TO MAKE THEM COOLER.

next: The Chief Chief

DID POWHATAN HELP JAMESTOWN?

THE MEETING OF **POWHATAN** AND **JOHN SMITH** AT **JAMESTOWN, VIRGINIA,** IS THE CLASH OF TWO CULTURES WITH IMPORTANT SIMILARITIES. . .

GOOD TRADERS

POWHATAN INDIANS TRADE CORN TO INDIANS ON THE EASTERN SHORE, ACROSS THE CHESAPEAKE BAY.

GOOD SAILORS

THESE FIRST AMERICANS BURN OUT TREES TO MAKE CANOES 50 FEET LONG. SOME CANOES CAN CARRY 40 MEN!

GOOD WARRIORS

THESE **ALGONQUIAN** SPEAKERS OFTEN RAID VILLAGES OF THE **SIOUAN** SPEAKERS IN WESTERN VIRGINIA.

GOOD TRADERS

THE VIRGINIA COMPANY OF LONDON IS SETTLING VIRGINIA AS AN **ECONOMIC** VENTURE. THE EXPLORERS ARE SUPPOSED TO FIND THINGS TO TRADE IN ENGLAND.

GOOD SAILORS

ENGLISHMEN ARE GOOD SAILORS BECAUSE ENGLAND IS AN ISLAND. THEIR TRADING SHIPS TRAVEL THOUSANDS OF MILES ACROSS OPEN OCEAN.

GOOD WARRIORS

THOUGH ENGLAND HAS NOT BEEN SUCCESSFULLY INVADED FOR CENTURIES, ENGLISHMEN ARE OFTEN AT WAR IN EUROPE.

I WILL HELP YOU IF **YOU** HELP DEFEND MY PEOPLE AGAINST THE SIOUAN-SPEAKING MONACANS FROM THE WESTERN MOUNTAINS.

WE HAVE ONLY 104 MEN, BUT WE DO HAVE GUNS AND CANNONS. WE NEED YOU TO SHOW US HOW TO GROW FOOD IN THIS PLACE.

BOYD '02

POWHATAN'S PEOPLE HELP JAMESTOWN SETTLERS SURVIVE THEIR FIRST HOT, HUMID DAYS.

THIS IS CALLED "CORN."

IS **THIS** THE NATION THAT WILL CONQUER ME? THESE MEN ARE TOO ILL TO DO MUCH! MANY OTHERS REFUSE TO WORK. WE COULD ATTACK THEM NOW AND WIPE THEM OUT!!

ON MAY 27, 1607, HUNDREDS OF POWHATAN WARRIORS ATTACK THE UNFINISHED JAMESTOWN FORT.

THEY FAIL. ENGLISH GUNS DRIVE THEM BACK.

next: OFF WITH HIS HEAD

DID POWHATAN TRY TO KILL SMITH?

RIGHT AFTER THE ENGLISH GOT TO JAMESTOWN, JOHN SMITH TOOK CHARGE OF GETTING FOOD. HE WENT TO THE **POWHATANS**. AND NOW WE WILL TOO!

WHERE ARE **YOU** GOING?

WE--WE'RE HERE TO ASK ABOUT JOHN SMITH.

SMITH THE TERRORIST?!!

ON SMITH'S FIRST TRADING VISIT TO THE KECOUGHTANS, WHO LIVE BY THE CHESAPEAKE BAY, HE KILLED INDIANS SO THE SURVIVORS WOULD GIVE HIM COR[N]

I HAVE SEEN SMITH CHAIN INDIANS AND FORCE THEM TO WORK. HE ONCE WHIPPED AN INDIAN.

WHEN WE GAVE HIM FOOD, HE WAS HAPPY. WHEN WE DID NOT, SMITH BURNED OUR VILLAGES.

BUT OUR LEADER, **POWHATAN**, DID NOT KILL SMITH. HE MADE SMITH A "WEROWANCE"— A SON!

BOYD '99

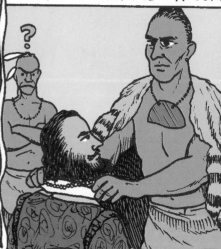

IS THAT BECAUSE **POCAHONTAS** WANTED HIM SAVED? WHAT ABOUT THAT STORY OF HER SAVING SMITH FROM BEING KILLED BY POWHATAN'S MEN?

PERHAPS IT IS JUST A STORY. I DO NOT KNOW.
YOU SHOULD ASK HER HUSBAND, JOHN ROLFE.

ROLFE?! I THOUGHT SHE LOVED SMITH!

NEXT:
STORM

16

HOW DID POCAHONTAS SAVE JAMESTOWN?

THE FIRST MONTHS OF THE ENGLISH SETTLEMENT AT **JAMESTOWN**, VIRGINIA, SEE SOME STRANGE TWISTS...

SOMETIMES THE ENGLISH TRADE WITH POWHATAN INDIANS IN PEACE.

I'LL GIVE YOU TWO POTS, A PITCHFORK, AND A GUN FOR YOUR CORN, THREE FURS, AND YOUR LEATHER CLOAK.

THROW IN A BASEBALL CARD— MAYBE A ROOKIE WILLIE MAIZE??

SOMETIMES THE ENGLISH AND POWHATANS AMBUSH EACH OTHER AND TAKE PRISONERS.

WE HAVE JOHN SMITH, THE ENGLISHMAN WHO BURNS OUR VILLAGES AND TAKES OUR CORN!!

STOP!

MOVE AWAY, POCAHONTAS!! I KILLED THE ENGLISH AT ROANOKE ISLAND, AND I WILL KILL THEM HERE!!

YOU MUST KILL **ME** FIRST!

LET HIM GO.

A FEW MONTHS LATER THE ENGLISH TAKE SEVEN INDIAN WARRIORS CAPTIVE.

MY DAD ASKS ME TO BRING THE MEN HOME WITH ME.

POWHATAN SENDS A 12-YEAR-OLD GIRL TO BARTER?!?

GIVE HER THE MEN— AND MANY GIFTS. I OWE MY LIFE TO HER.

IN JANUARY 1609, POCAHONTAS GOES THROUGH A SLEET STORM TO WARN JAMESTOWN.

BEWARE! MY DAD SENDS WARRIORS TO ATTACK YOU, JOHN SMITH!

POCAHONTAS' FRIENDSHIP WITH THE COLONISTS HELPS THEM SURVIVE.

I BELIEVE THE ENGLISH AND THE POWHATANS CAN LIVE IN PEACE.

next: Love & Marriage

WHO MARRIED POCAHONTAS?

IN THE FALL OF **1609**, JOHN SMITH LEAVES JAMESTOWN, VIRGINIA, AFTER A BAG OF GUNPOWDER ON HIS HIP BLOWS UP.

A YEAR AFTER SMITH RETURNS TO ENGLAND, THE 13-YEAR-OLD INDIAN NAMED POCAHONTAS MARRIES AN INDIAN NAMED KOCOUM.

MAY THE GREAT RABBIT QUIOQUASCACKE ALWAYS BRING US CORN AND SUN.

THEIR **RELIGION** SHOWS A RESPECT FOR **NATURE**. THEY HAVE LEGENDS OF GODS THAT TAKE THE FORM OF ANIMALS.

IN 1613, THE ENGLISH KIDNAP POCAHONTAS.

TO GET YOU BACK, YOUR DAD, POWHATAN, MUST GIVE US THE WEAPONS AND MEN HE TOOK FROM US!

OH WELL. I'VE GOT 39 OTHER KIDS. I'D RATHER KEEP ENGLISH GUNS!

POCAHONTAS SWITCHES TO CHRISTIANITY AND ADOPTS THE NAME "REBECCA."

I NOW PRONOUNCE REBECCA MARRIED TO TOBACCO WIZARD **JOHN ROLFE**.

ROLFE AND REBECCA HAVE A SON NAMED THOMAS. THE THREE OF THEM SAIL TO ENGLAND IN 1616. REBECCA BECOMES A CELBRITY AMONG THE RICH OF LONDON.

WE THINK SHE CATCHES SMALLPOX IN LONDON. JUST AS SHE SETS SAIL FOR VIRGINIA, SHE DIES AT AGE 22, IN **1617**. HER FATHER, POWHATAN, DIES IN 1618. IT IS A QUICK CLOSE TO THE FIRST CHAPTER OF ENGLISH AND INDIANS.

END

BOYD '02

NORTHWEST INDIANS

Some of the people who cross the Bering land bridge settle on the coast of the **Pacific Ocean**. In this area of the **American Northwest**, food is so easy to catch and shelter is so easy to make that the people have time to become great artists. From their villages rise the monuments we call totem poles . . .

WHERE DID KWAKIUTL INDIANS LIVE?

SAMUEL! LET'S TAKE A FIELD TRIP TO 1778.

COOL! COLONIAL AMERICA IS WILD. LET ME GET MY TRICORNER HAT.

WHA-?? WHERE IS GEORGE WASHINGTON?!

Pacific Ocean

TRIBES
☐ – TLINGIT
☐ – HAISLA
☐ – KWAKIUTL
☐ – NOOTKA
☐ – NEZ PERCE
☐ – COAST SALISH
☐ – CLATSOP

GEORGE IS ON THE ATLANTIC COAST OF NORTH AMERICA. WE ARE VISITING THE PACIFIC COAST! THIS IS A VILLAGE OF KWAKIUTL INDIANS ON VANCOUVER ISLAND.

THE KWAKIUTL (RHYMES WITH "YANKEE DOODLE") LIVE IN PLANK HOUSES MADE OF CEDAR LOGS. LOGS ARE EASY TO FIND HERE IN THICK FORESTS IN AMERICA'S NORTHWEST!

OK, SO IT IS LOGGY. WHY IS IT FOGGY?

WARM OCEAN BREEZES HIT THE MOUNTAINS AND DROP THEIR MOISTURE ONTO THE COASTAL FORESTS.

LOOK WHAT ELSE IS COMING IN FROM THE OCEAN!!

next: ROW, ROW, ROW

HOW DID KWAKIUTLS MAKE TOTEM POLES?

CHESTER, SAMUEL, AND ENGLISH EXPLORER JAMES COOK ARE VISITING **INDIANS** ON AMERICA'S **NORTHWEST COAST**...

THE MAST ON ONE OF MY SHIPS IS ROTTEN. HOW CAN WE REPLACE IT?

HEY!

WE KNOW WHERE THE TALLEST CEDAR TREES ARE. WE HAVE EXPERIENCE CUTTING THEM!

BECAUSE FOOD IS EASY TO FIND AROUND HERE, WE CAN SPEND MORE TIME MAKING ART. OUR FAVORITE ART FORM IS THE TOTEM POLE.

YOUR HAT IS NICE TOO.

IMPORTANT FAMILIES OWN TOTEM POLES, WHICH FEATURE THEIR ANCESTORS OR FAMILY SYMBOLS. IT CAN TAKE A YEAR TO CARVE AND PAINT A 60-FOOT POLE.

SOME POLES WELCOME VISITORS INTO A HOME. OTHERS ARE A MEMORIAL TO A DEAD PERSON. EACH ONE TELLS A STORY.

A TOY STORY?!

LET'S CARVE A SALMON IN YOUR MAST! THAT TELLS THE STORY OF WHERE YOU GOT IT!

UMM, NO THANKS.

next: POTLATCH LUCK

BOYD '02

WHAT IS A KWAKIUTL POTLATCH?

ENGLISH EXPLORER **JAMES COOK** IS READY TO LEAVE **AMERICA'S NORTHWEST COAST** IN 1778.

MY MASTS ARE REPAIRED. WE SET SAIL TOMOR—

WAIT!

WE MUST HAVE A GOODBYE **POTLATCH**!

A WHAT?!

A POTLATCH! KWAKIUTL AND NOOTKA INDIANS HAVE LARGE GATHERINGS THAT CAN BE A RELIGIOUS MEETING, A MEMORIAL TO THE DEAD, OR A CHANCE TO TRADE.

MORE TRADING?! IN TWO WEEKS HERE YOU HAVE STRIPPED MY SHIPS OF **ALL THEIR BRASS** (EXCEPT FOR MY VITAL INSTRUMENTS). MY OFFICERS HAVE **NO MORE BUTTONS** ON THEIR COATS!!

REPLACE THE COATS! WE HAVE CLOAKS MADE OF MOOSE AND BEAVER SKINS. SOMETIMES WE EVEN WEAVE GOAT HAIR INTO OUR CLOTHING!

COOK FINALLY AGREES TO GO TO THE POTLATCH.

WOW! THIS FUR WILL SELL FOR £2,000 IN EUROPE!

I LIKE THE DANCING. I WOULDN'T TRADE THIS FOR ANYTHING!

BYE! WE'LL SAY HI TO ICHIRO SUZUKI FOR YOU!

TODAY, NORTHWEST INDIANS STILL SING FAMILY SONGS TO THE BEAT OF A BOX DRUM AT POTLATCHES. END

BOYD '02